Olaus J. Murie   Marg

urie   ur

Olaus J. Murie   Marg

urie   Margaret E. Mur

Olaus J. Murie   Marg

urie   Margaret E. Mur

Olaus J. Murie   Marg

urie   Margaret E. Mur

Olaus J. Murie   Marg

urie   Margaret E. Mur

Olaus J. Murie   Marg

Murie   Margaret E. Mu

Margaret E. Murie   Olau

Murie   Margaret E. Mu

Margaret E. Murie   Olau

Murie   Margaret E. Mu

Margaret E. Murie   Olau

Murie   Margaret E. Mu

Margaret E. Murie   Olau

Murie   Margaret E. Mu

Margaret E. Murie   Olau

Murie   Margaret E. Mu

A SHORT BIOGRAPHY OF MARGARET AND OLAUS MURIE

A SHORT BIOGRAPHY OF

Margaret and Olaus Murie

Christen Girard

 **BENNA** BOOKS

Carlisle, Massachusetts

A Short Biography of Margaret and Olaus Murie

Series Editor: Susan DeLand
Written by: Christen Girard

Copyright © 2019 Applewood Books, Inc.

978-1-944038-64-9

FRONT COVER: *Mardy and Olaus at their ranch home in Moose*, 1953
Photographer unknown
Color photograph
Murie Collection of Teton Science Schools
(Murie Ranch, Moose, Wyoming)

BACK COVER: *Mardy and Olaus wrapped in furs on
their Alaskan honeymoon*, 1924
Photographer unknown
Sepia photograph
Murie Collection of Teton Science Schools
(Murie Ranch, Moose, Wyoming)

Published by Benna Books
an imprint of Applewood Books, Inc.
Carlisle, Massachusetts 01741

To request a free copy of our current catalog
featuring our best-selling books, write to:
Applewood Books, Inc.
P.O. Box 27
Carlisle, Massachusetts 01741
Or visit us on the web at: www.awb.com

10 9 8 7 6 5 4 3 2 1
MANUFACTURED IN THE UNITED STATES OF AMERICA

WRAPPED IN FURS WITH THEIR FOOD, bedding, research materials, and art supplies strapped to their dogsled, newlyweds Olaus and Margaret Murie made an epic 550-mile honeymoon journey through Arctic Alaska so that Olaus could continue his research on the caribou herds. It was on this first adventure together that Olaus recognized he had found a companion equally at home in nature as he, someone willing to endure the hardships of Arctic travel, and a partner who shared his love for the beauty of wild places. Thus began the

Muries' lives together. Their partnership demonstrated that one's life and work can be strengthened not just by another, but by a shared intimacy with the natural world gained only through deep and invigorating outdoor experiences. As pioneering scientists, naturalists, writers, artists, conservationists, and visionaries, Mardy and Olaus *lived* their work. This deep ethic embraced family, friends, and community, with nature at the center. During much of the twentieth century, the Muries worked tirelessly on behalf of wilderness and wildlife, helping to shape the modern conservation movement and influence a new era of thinking about the real purpose of nature in all its beautiful, untamed, infinite complexity.

The Muries' love for each other was rooted in wild country.

The early lives of Mardy and Olaus were shaped by innumerable experiences in the outdoors, Mardy in frontier Alaska and Olaus in northwestern Minnesota. This eagerness for adventure proved to be the foundation of the Muries' future life together. As a young girl, Mardy would take off on long walks where she spent hours poking around in the wild. Because of this, Mardy's stepfather teased her for being part gypsy, and yet he encouraged her young spirit: "Curiosity, that divine thing, curiosity. It will carry you on when all else fails." She never forgot his words, and they helped her through many challenges later in her life. Like Mardy, Olaus too was curious about everything around him. His boyhood was filled with adventures in the woods along the local Red River—fishing and swimming in summer, skating on frozen ponds in winter, camping and canoeing in the fall. He and his younger brothers built forts and tepees and practiced survival skills, encouraged by the books of naturalist Ernest Thompson Seton, founder of the Boy Scouts of America.

Olaus Johan Murie was born on March 1, 1889, in Moorehead, Minnesota, to Norwegian immigrants Joachim Murie and Marie Frimanslund Murie. Joachim died when Olaus was seven

"There were woods, birds, mammals. It was living close to the earth—you know what that does to you." — OJM

and his brother, Martin, was four. Marie remarried a Swedish immigrant named Ed Wickstrom several years later, and they had a son named Adolph. Ed died two years after that, leaving Marie nearly penniless again with three boys to raise in a small frame house surrounded by prairie. To support her family, Marie washed laundry and cleaned the church, and she cut grass with a hand scythe to feed their cow. The boys took jobs delivering milk, working at the local farm, and collecting firewood to supplement their mother's meager income.

Still, Olaus loved his childhood. Encouraged by his mother, he read a lot of books, including those by Seton and other naturalists such as John Burroughs. In addition to seeking outdoor adventures, he enjoyed drawing as a means of connecting to his surroundings. Although Olaus took only one art class in school, he had natural talent, and his eighth-grade teacher, Miss King, encouraged his artistic abilities. As a scientist years later, Olaus was known to

Martin, who became a biologist like his brother Olaus, died in 1922 from tuberculosis.

carry drawing paper in the back of his field notebook, completing detailed sketches of the scenery and specimens he studied with scientific accuracy. These drawings often accompanied his technical field reports sent to supervisors in Washington, D.C., and were also included in many of the books the Muries published over the years.

Peterson's Field Guide to Animal Tracks, originally written and illustrated by Olaus in 1954, includes over 1,000 line drawings of wildlife tracks and patterns.

"I have always had a strong feeling for color, whether in the sky or in the earthy landscape." — OJM

Margaret Elizabeth Thomas (Mardy) was born on August 18, 1902, in Seattle, Washington. Her parents, Minnie Eva Fraser and Ashton Wayman Thomas, both moved west to Washington State from Grand Manan Island, New Brunswick, in the 1880s in order to see the world and to create a new life. Ashton worked on boats in Elliott Bay, served for a short time as sheriff of San Juan County, and then opened a fish cannery at Friday Harbor in the San Juan Islands of the Puget Sound.

As an enterprising businessman, years later he successfully opened a second cannery in Prince William Sound, Alaska, where Mardy would spend many summers as a young adult learning to catch and process fish and exploring numerous coastal inlets.

Just after Mardy was born, the family moved to Juneau, Alaska, but by the time she was five her parents had divorced and Mardy returned to Seattle with her mother. Back on the mainland, Minnie put herself through business school. Three years later she married a lawyer working for the federal court system, Louis Gillette, who was assigned a position back in Fairbanks, Alaska. And so Mardy returned to the wilds of her early childhood in 1911, to a town where mail still arrived by dogsled, saloons on street corners outnumbered churches, and a trip to the city took three weeks by steamer, train, and horse-drawn cart. She loved the free and simple life that Fairbanks, at the edge of civilization, offered. It required self-discipline, a

Frontier Alaska would not become a state until 1959.

strong character, and equal measures of grit and humor. Daily routine helped, and Mardy learned to bake molasses cookies, making them each Saturday while her mother made pies and doughnuts.

As the eldest siblings in their families, Mardy and Olaus were mentor figures to their younger brothers and sisters. Adolph Murie followed closely in Olaus' footsteps, becoming a renowned biologist working for the Park Service in Mt. McKinley (now Denali) and Yellowstone National Parks. Throughout his career, Adolph fought against the eradication of large carnivores and wrote several books articulating the importance of predators in the ecosystem. Mardy's half-siblings Louise, Louis, and Carol were raised to have the same wild and adventurous Alaskan spirit that governed their big sister. Louise (Weezy), in particular, took after Mardy in her love of nature. She studied botany at Reed College, becoming an accomplished botanist and field scientist and keeping a lifelong

Adolph's research on wolves and grizzlies provides some of the most well-articulated and vital insights into predator-prey relationships in modern ecology.

connection to Alaska as well. To prove just how closely the younger siblings emulated the actions of their elders, Adolph Murie and Weezy eventually married each other in Jackson Hole in 1932 at the home of Mardy and Olaus. They had initially become acquainted in Alaska while the Murie brothers were studying caribou migrations in the early 1920s.

Perhaps as a lesson learned from the hardships she had endured in her own life, Marie Murie always encouraged her sons to get an education. In 1908, Olaus received a scholarship from Fargo College in North Dakota, enabling him to attend for one year. He then transferred to Pacific University in Oregon, taking jobs washing dishes, doing laundry, and assisting in the biology lab to get through school. Between classes, Olaus participated on the cross-country running and track teams. One season he played football as a line guard despite only weighing 135 pounds. Years later, Olaus would recall those days fondly as a time when he first learned the

Olaus traveled by train to Oregon with only a sack lunch and a few clothes.

importance of maintaining physical health alongside intellectual activity for the well-being of a person's spirit.

Olaus graduated in 1912 with a biology degree and immediately started working as a naturalist for the Oregon Game Warden. After two years, he took a job with the Carnegie Museum of Natural History to have adventures and explore more of the world. Olaus' first expeditions to study nature and collect specimens, mostly birds, led him into the Canadian Arctic. When WWI broke out, he took a break from field work to serve in the Balloon Service of the Army Air Corps. After the war, Olaus accepted a new position as field biologist for the U.S. Fish and Wildlife Service (then the U.S. Biological Survey) in Alaska. He traveled into the far north country mainly to study the caribou herds and track their migrations and life histories, completing this exhausting research by dogsled. Along the way, he sketched everything he observed, adding color, beauty, and

Olaus found that outdoor life suited him and appreciated the hardships of long days spent traveling, hunting, and studying nature.

emotion to the wildness around him.

After graduating from high school, Mardy attended Reed College in Oregon. During the summers, she continued to seek adventure in Prince William Sound while working as the storekeeper at her father's cannery. When Mardy's father moved his family to Boston, Mardy decided to transfer to Simmons College there to enjoy the close camaraderie of family. Despite her caring and community-minded nature, Mardy felt isolated from her classmates, who often referred to her as "that girl from Alaska." And so, when Ashton Thomas unexpectedly returned to Seattle due to poor health, Mardy decided to finish the year at Simmons and then put her studies on hold to move back to Fairbanks where friends, family, and romance awaited her.

Olaus and Mardy were first introduced in the summer of 1921. On a resupply break between expeditions, Olaus and Adolph were renting a cabin down the street from the Gillette family home, and the brothers were invited to a neighbor's dinner party, which Mardy also attended. Although they exchanged only a few words during that first meeting, over the next several weeks the pair began an unusual acquaintance. One evening at a riverside camp they'd made with friends, Olaus called in a great horned owl and then sketched an image of the bird for Mardy. This made an impression on her. He was not like other men she had met in college. He was quiet and sweet, and she enjoyed the sound of his voice. At Christmastime during their first year of friendship, Mardy once became exasperated with Olaus' constant pleasantness and proclaimed, "Oh, what everlasting good nature!" To which he replied, "Look, if you want a fight, you can have it." She recognized then that, beneath his calm and unassuming nature, this man had a fighting spirit. When Olaus returned to his caribou research in the field that spring, the two agreed to stay in touch.

For those first months, the two wrote

Olaus did not know how to dance when the couple first met, so Mardy, who adored dancing, taught him to the tune of the "Hesitation Waltz."

each other letters. Mardy was back in school again, this time at the University of Alaska, which had just opened the year before. Mardy sent letters ahead of Olaus on his expeditions, and Olaus responded as he could between outpost camps and resupply stations with his dogsled team.

Olaus' letters would often arrive in cherished bundles, three or four at a time.

Through this correspondence, the pair shared the wonders and hardship of expeditions, the challenges of passing calculus class, and the joys of community dances. Finally, after a short visit together in the summer of 1923, Mardy and Olaus knew they would be married. The couple decided that Mardy should first finish her degree. The University of Alaska did not have an English major, but it did offer a degree in business, which Mardy had taken a few classes in while at Simmons College. And so, in 1924, Mardy became the first female graduate of the university and the only senior to graduate that year.

After graduation, Mardy traveled 800 miles down the Yukon River with her mother and friends, joyously reuniting with Olaus in Anvik, Alaska, on August 18, 1924—her birthday. Olaus had been unable to attend Mardy's graduation because he was on a five-month expedition studying waterfowl in the Bering Sea. The couple married at three o'clock that morning in a small riverside chapel and immediately departed on a three-month honeymoon, traveling by boat and dogsled into the Alaska Brooks Range. Olaus needed to complete his caribou research that winter, and Mardy, now a biologist's wife, would accompany him. During the trip, Olaus introduced Mardy to the intricacies of field research and taught her how to identify the flora and fauna of the region. This first magical journey together strengthened their love not only for each other, but for northern Alaska.

During the Muries' honeymoon adventure, Olaus recognized that Mardy shared equally his love of wilderness and adventure.

When the Muries returned from their honeymoon, they moved for a short time to Washington, D.C., near the U.S. Biological Survey headquarters. By the following summer, Mardy was pregnant and Olaus, away on a six-month research trip to study brown bears along the Alaskan peninsula, missed the birth of their first child, Martin, on July 10, 1925. Olaus was then assigned an expedition to study waterfowl along the Old Crow River in northeastern Alaska. Refusing to be a wife that stayed behind while her husband went off to have all the adventures, Mardy joined him. In the late spring of 1926, Olaus, Mardy, their good friend Jess Rust, and ten-month-old Martin traveled by motorboat to the headwaters of the Old Crow. About a month into the journey, the engine of their motorboat died and the group had to pole the boat another 250 miles upstream. This, coupled with the relentless mosquitoes and relatively few waterfowl actually observed, made the trip challenging. Despite the hardships, there were powerful moments of beauty too, and the trip deepened the Muries' love for the untouched wildlands of Alaska. This trip also established another important milestone: when Olaus went into the field on one of his research trips, the family would be coming along too.

Martin's playhouse was a big wooden box built especially for him in the boat.

In 1927, Olaus completed his master's degree from the University of Michigan and at the same time was given an assignment to study the life history of the North American elk herd in Jackson, Wyoming, which were dying mysteriously. Mardy, Martin, and the Muries' second child, daughter Joanne, born on May 21 of that year, joined Olaus in Wyoming. The family built a home in town but spent summers in the hills and sagelands living alongside the elk and tracking their movements, behaviors, and habits. Because Mardy often accompanied Olaus into the field, her contributions to Olaus' field research were substantial. She collected data and made observations alongside other trained technicians, recording these notes with scientific accuracy just as Olaus had taught her. Mardy had established herself as Olaus' secretary, a role she kept throughout all of her husband's technical, and later philosophical, career as a conservationist and wilderness advocate.

On December 16, 1931, the Muries' third child, Donald, was born.

"When we attain a new understanding of something in the field of science, the thoughtful scientist is filled with wonder and a degree of reverence for what we only partially understand. A poetic appreciation of life, combined with a knowledge of nature, creates humility, which in turn becomes the greatness of man." — OJM

As Olaus grew in his career, some of his ideas on wildlife management were starting to put him at odds with other federal scientists. Decades of field research had given him insights into how natural systems worked, and he published scientific papers arguing for the protection of all species in the food chain to maintain the functioning of the larger ecosystem. Olaus had witnessed these truths as a naturalist and field scientist, and he disagreed with the dominant beliefs that large predators and rodents were detrimental to the health of the environment or to populations of big game. Several of his technical papers were publicly criticized both within the agency and within the scientific community at large. At a time when it would have been easier to agree with the wisdom of agency policies governing wildlife management, Olaus stood by his science. His holistic assessment of ecological systems is now the cornerstone of modern conservation efforts.

By the mid-1930s, Olaus had reached the peak of his career as a scientist. His extensive research on the elk herds, accompanied by years of successful campaigning on their behalf, led to the expansion of the mammal's winter range at the southern end of the Jackson Hole valley. During these years, Olaus began meeting with many politicians and conservation thinkers, exploring ideas for an expanded Grand Teton National Park adjacent to Yellowstone National Park and the National Elk Refuge. While his ideas were not very popular during

Olaus called for tolerance of all species, articulating a nascent environmental ethic echoed today in endangered species protection.

that era of frontierism and western expansion, they propelled Olaus into new territory as an advocate for wildlife alongside public lands protection. He and Mardy formed an easy friendship with conservationist Bob Marshall, who had first heard of the Muries during his own travels through Koyukuk country in Alaska years before. In 1935 Marshall, along with Olaus and other visionaries, formed the Wilderness Society.

Mardy maintained her role as Olaus' secretary within the organization, where the Muries were respected for their years of experience living close to nature.

Olaus was offered the position of director (and later president) of the Wilderness Society after Marshall passed away. This new role was timely, as Olaus was ready to retire formally as a federal biologist and eager to dedicate more of his time to naturalist studies and protecting wildlife and their habitats. Mardy described this change:

> *"It seemed as though our lives just blossomed. [Olaus] felt free to do what he wanted to do. He felt his study of animals had*

reached a point where he was more concerned with trying to preserve their habitat than with doing more studies of them." — MEM

The Muries were also ready for a quieter life. For many years, they had been friends with the Estes family who ran a dude ranch north of Jackson in Moose, Wyoming, at the base of the Teton Mountains. When the Esteses decided to sell their ranch in 1945, Mardy and Olaus, along with Adolf and Weezy, purchased the property. The first thing the Muries did was remove all the fences so that wildlife could move about without hindrance.

The Muries threw themselves into their work with the Wilderness Society. They held society meetings at their ranch home, hosting every conservationist and wilderness thinker of the era, including Aldo Leopold, Sigurd Olson, and Howard Zahniser. Due to his achievements as a scientist and conservationist, Olaus was awarded a doctorate of science

In 1948, Olaus received a Fulbright Grant to study the elk herds in New Zealand, and Mardy and their son Donald accompanied him.

from his alma mater, Pacific University. Busy as ever, in 1956 he and Mardy led a scientific expedition with three other young biologists, Bob Krear, Brina Kessel, and George Shaller, to survey the upper Sheenjek River, a remote region of northeastern Alaska. This expedition was one of the best times of their lives—the Muries were back in nature together, and returning to the Arctic felt like coming home.

Back in Moose, the Muries summarized their findings through written and visual reports. Olaus gave talks and lectures and attended society meetings, where he discussed the need for formal protection of that vast wilderness area, a region many felt was under threat as Alaska achieved statehood. Olaus continued to find time for writing and painting and Mardy worked alongside as his secretary. Finally, in 1960, the Arctic National Wildlife Refuge was established. When the Muries received word that 8 million acres of their beloved Arctic had been protected by executive

In 1963, Mardy published *Two in the Far North*, chronicling her journeys in the Arctic with Olaus and other companions.

order, they wept for joy, considering this the happiest achievement of their lives.

While the Muries were fighting tirelessly on behalf of Alaska, Olaus was struggling with a personal battle. He became ill with tuberculosis in 1954, the same disease that his brother, Martin, had died of three decades earlier. He was later diagnosed with melanoma, and by 1962 his cancer was progressing. Still, Olaus continued his work. He was honored with several major conservation awards, including the Wildlife Society Award (1951), the Aldo Leopold Memorial Medal (1952), the Audubon Medal (1959), and the John Muir Award from the Sierra Club (1963). The Muries made two more trips to Alaska, the first in 1961 back to the Sheenjek and another in the summer of 1963 to attend a Wilderness Society meeting and connect with Adolph and Weezy, studying wolves in Mt. McKinley National Park. Back home in Jackson that fall, Olaus passed away at a hospital on October 21, 1963.

Howard Zahniser, who wrote the 1964 Wilderness Act, fondly remembered Olaus as the person who best personified wilderness in American culture.

After an amazing thirty-nine-year adventure together, Mardy was heartbroken. Unable to remain in Wyoming, where so many reminders of her beloved existed, she spent that first winter in Seattle with her mother. When she finally found the courage to return to their ranch home, it was as if the cabin enveloped her a warm embrace. Mardy realized then what she must do. To honor Olaus' spirit, she would dedicate herself to continuing his conservation work. Mardy began writing letters and articles, lobbying and lecturing across the country and testifying in front of Congress on behalf of wilderness. On September 3, 1964, less than one year after Olaus passed away, President Lyndon B. Johnson signed the Wilderness Act into law.

Mardy attended the signing of the Wilderness Act, where the Muries' dream of a comprehensive law protecting wildlands finally came true.

For the next forty years, Mardy continued to give voice to the lands that she and Olaus loved. In 1975 she returned to Alaska, accompanied by good friends Celia Hunter and Dr. Brina Kessel. They surveyed lands for inclusion in the proposed Alaska

National Interest Lands Conservation Act (ANILCA). She had many adventures on that trip, including the difficult landing of the prop plane they were flying for aerial surveys after its engine lost power. This trip was demonstrative of just how influential Mardy had become. She knew Alaska intimately, understood the science of the Arctic, and was a core member of the Wilderness Society. These attributes made her the perfect voice for conservation.

By the 1980s, Mardy was considered by many to be the grandmother of the American conservation movement.

Though initially reticent to give speeches, Mardy gradually grew more confident and assured. She believed that there was always something more to strive for when it came to the fight for wild country. Her influence as a spokesperson was strengthened by the emotional connection to nature she had cultivated all her life and which pervaded her work. After returning from that 1975 Alaska trip, Mardy gave a powerful speech before Congress:

> *"I am testifying as an emotional woman and I would like to ask*

*you, gentlemen, what is wrong
with emotion? Beauty is a resource
in and of itself. Alaska must be
allowed to be Alaska, that is her
greatest economy. I hope the
United States of America is not so
rich that she can afford to let those
wildernesses pass by, nor so poor
she cannot afford to keep them."*
— *MEM*

As a result of her efforts, and those of many others, ANILCA was finally passed in 1980, setting aside an additional 56 million acres of wilderness in the far north.

Like Olaus, Mardy received an honorary doctorate and many conservation awards, including the Presidential Medal of Freedom (1998), the nation's highest civilian honor, at the age of ninety-six.

The Murie Ranch remained a convening place for people involved in the conservation movement for many decades; everyone from politicians to writers and teachers to students came to visit. As had been a family tradition since growing up in Alaska, Mardy was always ready with homemade cookies. Countless young people were profoundly affected by meetings with Mardy and, in earlier years, with Olaus. Throughout his life, Olaus had championed getting youth outdoors into the freedom of wilderness, where they could experience the woods, water, and wild creatures. To him, the real purpose of the outdoors was to experience a world full of life, beauty, and joy. Mardy too was an advocate for education and had great faith in the younger generation. She strongly advised youth, as future leaders of the environmental movement, to get outside to explore and engage with the world. Indeed, their own children, Martin, Joanne, and Don, having grown up close to nature, each followed their hearts and continued to foster these connections in their own ways: Martin as a college biology professor, Joanne as a mother, and Don through photography and as a filmmaker.

Mardy, Adolph, and Weezy sold their ranch home to the National Park Service in 1968 in order to create a contiguous Grand Teton National Park, and they continued to live there with long-term leases. Mardy took an active role in education efforts, becoming a founding board member of the Teton Science Schools in 1967, a place-based nonprofit education organization in Jackson Hole, and later supporting the creation of an organization to carry on the Muries' conservation vision, the Murie Center. For many years, the center stewarded the spiritual values of wild places and eventually merged with the Teton Science Schools in 2015, which continues to steward the ranch, the Murie legacy, and the next generation of conservation leaders.

After Adolph passed away in 1977, Weezy moved off the ranch and took up residence in the town of Jackson.

Mardy passed away quietly at her home in Moose on October 19, 2003, at the age of 101. She and Olaus are remembered for their incalculable impact on the American conservation movement—crusaders for the right of all people to enjoy wilderness and the right of all wild species to do the same. Throughout their lives, the Muries kept faith in wild places, and they kept profound faith in people too. Their extraordinary, entwined story of love and commitment to people and place is a testament to the power that individuals can have when they have the courage to follow what they know to be true. The Muries led by example. They lived their work. They fought hard, kept their senses of humor and, at the end of the day, they always remembered to dance.

In 2006, the Murie Ranch was federally designated a National Historic Landmark.